Gard... of the...

Written by Jo Windsor

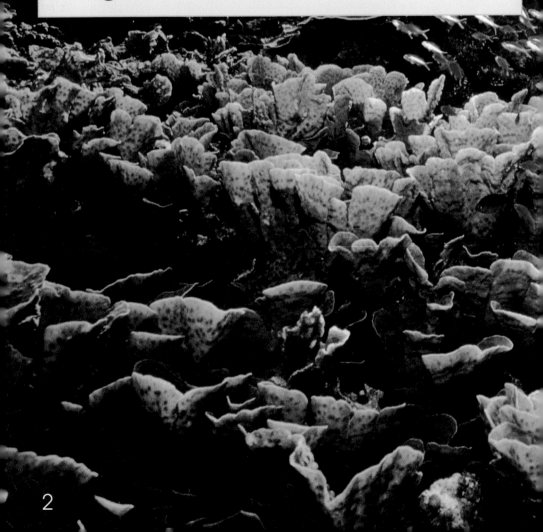

Some parts of the sea
are like gardens.
Animals can live in
these gardens and
get food from them.

Animals can live and feed in the gardens of coral.

Coral can grow in lots of shapes.
Some shapes look like fingers.
Some shapes look like leaves.
Some shapes look like fans.

Divers dive down
into the coral reefs.
They can see all the
animals that live in
the coral.

Sea grass grows
in the gardens
of the sea, too.
This octopus
eats the sea grass.

This dugong likes to eat
the sea grass, too.
It pulls up
the roots of the sea grass
and eats them.

Seaweed grows in the
gardens of the sea, too.
This seaweed is called kelp.
It can grow into a big forest.

The sea otters can dive
down into the seaweed
to get food.

People can get seaweed
from the gardens of the sea, too.
They can use the seaweed
for food.

These people are eating sushi.
Sushi is made of rice, fish,
vegetables and seaweed.

What can you see in the gardens of the sea?

Index

▬▬ Guide Notes

Title: Gardens of the Sea
Stage: Early (4) – Green

Genre: Non-Fiction
Approach: Guided Reading
Processes: Thinking Critically, Exploring Language, Processing Information
Visual Focus: Photographs (static images), Index

THINKING CRITICALLY
(sample questions)
- What do you think this book is going to tell us?
- What do you see on the front cover? What does this tell us about the sea?
- Focus the children's attention on the Index. Ask: "What animals and things are you going to find out about in this book?"
- If you want to find out about an octopus, what page would you look on?
- If you want to find out about seaweed, what page would you look on?
- If you want to find out about sushi, what page would you look on?
- Look at pages 4 and 5. Describe the different shapes of coral you can see.
- Look at pages 6 and 7. Why do you think the people have diving gear?
- Look at pages 8 and 9. What do you think these animals like to eat?

EXPLORING LANGUAGE

Terminology
Title, cover, illustrations, photographs, author, illustrator, photographers, title page, index

Vocabulary
Interest words: coral, fans, divers, dugongs, kelp, forest, sushi
High-frequency words (new): use, these
Compound word: seaweed

Print Conventions
Capital letter for sentence beginnings and title, full stops, commas, question mark